# Fun Facts About

# Axolotl

*47 Frequently Asked Questions by Axolotl Pet Owners and Lovers - Short Info Book for Kids*

*FIONA WEBER*

# INTRODUCTION

Are you in search of a unique but manageable pet?
Then go for an axolotl. No, this is not a typo, these
beauties really are called that. Say 'axe a lottle' and
you've nailed it. Be it its name, appearance, or
qualities, an axolotl takes ten on ten for its
uniqueness quotient. Axolotls belong to the
salamander family. Their face looks like a smiley's
been perpetually drawn on it and they have tiny
hands and feet which give them the name 'walking
fish'. However, they are amphibians with the ability
to breathe out of water albeit for a very short
period. Named after the Aztec god of fire and
lightning they have the distinctive ability to
regenerate lost limbs and even organs like the heart,
and brain. They live for quite a long and are
relatively easy to care for. Interested? Then go
ahead and read this book because any question that
comes to your mind regarding axolotls and we've
already answered

# 1. What is an axolotl?

Named after the Aztec god of fire and lightning, the axolotl is a remarkable species from the salamander family. It has two tiny legs and two tiny feet and a face like a smiley, 'grinning from ear to ear'. It also has feathery gills and a long, quill-like dorsal fin. An axolotl displays these tadpole-like features because of a rare condition called 'neoteny' due to which it retains all the features of its larval stage even when fully mature. But these Mexican amphibians have another quality that has attracted and baffled scientists ever since it was first discovered. It has the ability to regenerate lost limbs or organs which means they can grow another limb or organ and stay 'young' for life.

# 2. How do you say Axolotl?

These creatures may have a fancy name but it's quite easy to pronounce once you know how. Just say 'axe a lottle' and you'll be right on the mark. Or alternately, pronounce it as ACK-suh-LAH-tuhl

# 3. What is the scientific name of axolotl?

In scientific terms, an axolotl is known as Ambystoma mexicanum. It literally means 'Mexican Salamander.

## 4. Which animal group does the axolotl belong to?

The Axolotl is an amphibian. It was first discovered in Lake Xochimilco which lies beneath Mexico City and other nearby lakes. Even as an amphibian, it is unique because it does not go through metamorphosis to reach adulthood. Rather, it retains the features of its juvenile stage. It lives in the water throughout its life and can breathe out of it for a very short period.

## 5. What climate do axolotls live in?

Axolotls were found exclusively in Lake Xochimilco and surrounding lakes. But today, only Lake Xochimilco remains a relic of its previous glorious state, mainly due to the urbanization of Mexico City. Wild axolotls are found exclusively in the lake and the swampy canals that lead off the main body of the lake. The water temperature in Xochimilco remains mostly constant at 20 degrees Celsius (68 degrees Fahrenheit) although it can drop several degrees in winter.

## 6. Why is the axolotl not a fish?

Imagine a fish-like creature with tiny hands and legs and funny feathery things sticking out from both sides of its head swimming in the water. No wonder it's commonly known as the 'walking fish'. But surprisingly, the axolotl is not a fish but an amphibian from the salamander group. Amphibians are a group of animals that can live on both land and water. They have lungs to breathe through. So does the axolotl.  It has gills as well. The feathery things that stick out of an axolotl's head are actually gills.

## 7. When was the axolotl first discovered?

Centuries ago, in the 1200s, the Mexican Valley was settled by the Aztec people. They built their capital around the lakes that were home to the axolotl. When they discovered this peculiar creature, they named it after their god of fire and lightning. The axolotl usually made its home in rotting wood and when the wood was thrown in the fire, a wriggling salamander would emerge from it. This led to the belief that axolotls were born from fire.

## 8. What are the types of axolotls?

Axolotl numbers are dwindling in the wild but its popularity as a pet has led to extensive breeding in captivity. As a result, many different color morphs have emerged. As a potential axolotl pet owner, you have a range of around fifteen colors to choose from. The rarity of its color morph determines the axolotl's value, among other things.

· Leucistic: translucent white with golden flecks and dark eyes

· Golden Albino: shades range from almost white to orange-gold

· Wild Type: dark mottled shades of grey, green or black

· Piebald: white with dark patches on the face

· Mosaic: rare accidental color morph of mottled black, white and golden flecks with multi-colored eyes

· Copper: light gray bodies with copper-colored freckles

· Lavender: light, silvery purple with grey spots

· Black Melanoid: dark green to black

· White Albino: pure white with pink or white eyes

· Speckled Leucistic: a light spattering of dark green, brown, or black on a white base

· Chimera: another rare accident with the body split into two by two different color morph

· Heavily-Marked Melanoid: black with light green and yellow patches

· Green Fluorescent Protein: display a fluorescent glow when seen under ultraviolet light

· Firefly: dark with green fluorescent tails

· Enigma: dark grey with greenish-golden patches

## 9. Which type of axolotl is the rarest?

The rarest types of axolotls are the Chimera,

Mosaic, Piebald Enigma, Firefly, and Lavender, with Chimera and Mosaic being accidental morphs that cannot be bred.

## 10. What colors do axolotls come in?

To understand colors, we must first understand pigments. An axolotl has three types of pigment cells and its color morphs are created by playing around with these three pigments in the laboratory. Common colors create basic morphs. Uncommon colors create special morphs and very uncommon colors create rare morphs.

The basic morphs are leucistic, albino, axanthic, and melanoid.

Uncommon morphs are the glow-in-the-dark green and the copper axolotl.

rare morphs, which are near-impossible to get hold of, are, chimera, piebald, mosaic, silver dalmatian, enigma, and firefly.

## 11. How big does an axolotl grow?

An average length for an axolotl is 20 cm or 9 inches. However, it could grow up to 18 inches or 40 cm. An axolotl has a broad, flat body with toed limbs projecting out from the body at right angles and feather-like gills on its head.

## 12. Are axolotls dangerous?

Axolotls are not dangerous to human beings. However, they are carnivores and cannibals too. They will eat smaller fish and nibble on the body parts of other axolotls if they sense danger.

## 13. Describe the life-cycle of an axolotl.

Axolotls reach maturity by six months. Their breeding season lasts from December till June. They breed at least once during this season. The female lays eggs and right after laying eggs, the axolotl begins to reproduce again without a break. The female can lay up to 1000 eggs. The young axolotl grows very fast and reaches maturity by six months.

## 14. When do axolotl eggs hatch?

When kept at a higher end of the safe temperature range, around 72F, axolotl eggs will hatch in 15 days. It would be a good idea to remove the eggs as soon as they are hatched as axolotls don't mind eating their own eggs.

## 15. How long does it take an axolotl to become fully grown?

By six months, an axolotl is fully grown.

## 16. How long do axolotls live?

On average, an axolotl lives for 12-15 years.

## 17. Can the axolotl reach the final salamander stage of growth?

An axolotl can be forced to metamorphosize into a salamander by giving it iodine, but it would be an unnatural and short life.

## 18. Do axolotls have personalities?

Axolotls are goofy and weird and this gives them a funny personality.

## 19. What is unique about the axolotl larva?

It shows signs of neoteny and an absence of thyroxine which hinders metamorphosis.

## 20. Would axolotls make good pets?

Axolotls make for wonderful pets, as they are friendly and relatively easy to care for. With care, they can live for long.

## 21. Are axolotls hard to take care of?

They are not at all hard to care for. Their needs are quite straightforward and would make a good choice for beginners. However, they do require a water tank with a controlled temperature to thrive.

## 22. How much does an axolotl cost?

The regular variety cost between $30 – $75 while an exotic variety, like the piebald, may cost $100.

## 23. Are axolotls illegal?

It is illegal to own an axolotl in many parts of the US including California, Maine, New Jersey, Virginia, and D.C., while in Mexico and Hawaii a permit is needed. In Canada, New Brunswick, British Columbia, and Prince Edward Island deem it illegal, while Nova Scotia demands a permit.

## 24. Why are axolotls illegal?

Axolotls have been deemed illegal to protect their numbers from decreasing even more. along with protecting the axolotl, it also protects the local ecosystem by not letting the species die out.

## 25. Why are axolotls endangered?

Water pollution, urbanization, and natural causes have led to the loss of habitat. The axolotl's demand in the aquarium trade has led it into the critically endangered list.

## 26. How many axolotls are left?

Habitat loss has depleted axolotl numbers to only between 700 and 1,200 axolotls in the wild.

## 27. What is special about an axolotl?

Just like we regrow our nails and hair after it has been cut, an axolotl can regrow or regenerate missing limbs, kidneys, heart, lungs, and even its brain. Because of this ability, scientists have been using it for years to learn more about its regenerative ability.

## 28. Are axolotls really immortal?

No, they aren't. They have the remarkable ability to regenerate lost limbs and organs and because of this people sometimes associate them with mythical creatures. Rest assured, the axolotl will die of old age when it's time.

## 29. Do axolotls bite?

Yes, they do! Their teeth are too small to cause pain although they bite into anything that comes near them. They aren't dangerous to human beings, they bite out of curiosity or self-defense.

## 30. How do axolotls get energy?

The axolotl is a carnivore. Wild axolotls will eat worms, small fish, and anything else that they can. However, as pets, they eat worms and fish pellets.

## 31. What do axolotl like to eat?

Axolotls are happy to eat anything fed to them. They are not fussy about their food. Some of the safer and tastier snacks include:

· Bloodworms

· Frozen Brine

· Live Nightcrawlers Mysis Shrimp

· Red Wigglers

· Small Bits of Raw, Lean Beef Heart

## 32. When do axolotl feed?

Young axolotls need food daily, whereas adult axolotls require food 2-3 times a week. During the other days, they digest their food. A comfortable and smart way to feed them is by lightly dropping the food in the water, using forceps.

## 33. How long can an axolotl go without eating?

An axolotl can usually survive for up to 3 weeks without food without any long-term effects. However, the water temperature should not exceed 61F.

## 34. What happens if you put iodine on an axolotl?

When axolotls are administered the required amount of iodine in a controlled environment, it induces the production of thyroxine. As a result, metamorphosis may occur and the axolotl may move out of its larval stage into the adult stage. However, this cannot be tried at home as iodine is extremely toxic and dangerous for the axolotl.

## 35. Who are an axolotl's enemies?

The axolotl has few enemies in the wild. Storks and herons may make a meal out of them or they may be taken by larger fish like carp and tilapia. But urbanization and water pollution remain their biggest threat.

## 36. What kind of tank do axolotls need?

A standard 2ft (61cm) tank is quite adequate for one or two axolotls allowing them enough room to swim about. Avoid gravel to prevent choking. Fine sand and one or two hides will be a good choice for your axolotl tank.

## 37. How cold do axolotls like their water?

For an axolotl, ideal living conditions consist of water temperature which is constant between 60-64° F (16-18° C). They may require a chiller in warmer weather. It is preferable to keep the tank away from direct sunlight to prevent temperature fluctuation and the growth of algae.

## 38. Do axolotls need hides?

Yes, Axolotls do need hides as they like dark environments. A hide allows them to de-stress and relax. There should be plenty of space and 1-2 hides big enough to accommodate the axolotl's whole body.

## 39. Can you hold an axolotl in your hand?

Axolotls do not like being held at all. They become stressed and try to escape which may cause one or more of their delicate limbs to get damaged or break. So, do not pick up your axolotl unless it is urgent or necessary, like tank cleaning or giving medicine.

## 40. For how long can an axolotl remain out of water?

Axolotls are neotenic, which means they stopped

changing after the larval stage. This is why they are more aquatic than terrestrial. They can breathe out of water for only a short while. They must remain in the water to allow them to breathe properly. They can die if taken out of water even for a few minutes.

## 41. Will an axolotl die in cold water?

Axolotls are poikilothermic, which means their body temperature is the same as the temperature of the water surrounding them. They cannot survive in freezing temperatures.

## 42. How do axolotl sleep?

Since an axolotl does not have eyelids, it is challenging to really know if your axolotl is sleeping. It is crepuscular, which means it will sleep in the dark, night hours, and nap in the daytime. You can tell whether your axolotl is sleeping by the time of day and its frequency of movement. When at rest, it usually retreats to its hiding spots, remains still, and its gill movement also slows down. It also becomes paler when it is asleep.

## 43. Do axolotl die easily?

Axolotls live a long life. If all things go well, they should live a happy fifteen years on average. There are some factors that can cause its death before its time. These can be easily avoided by being careful and alert. Poor water quality is a very common oversight that can cost you your axolotl's health or life. Change your tank water regularly to remove harmful toxins. High ammonia levels can kill your axolotl. Make sure your tank's water is cycled and maintained at the temperature appropriate for an axolotl (60-64° Fahrenheit/16-18° Celsius). Keeping your water clean and fresh will also reduce the chances of parasites, infections, or impaction. What is impaction? It is when something gets stuck inside the axolotl's gut and can cause bloating and death. Do ensure your tank is free from big pieces of gravel too. Is your axolotl being fed well? Inadequate feeding can also cause stress and invite infections. If you ticked all the boxes and still your axolotl died, then maybe it's a case of poor genes.

## 44. Can axolotl live with other fish?

Axolotl can live with other fishes or freshwater creatures, but not for long; one or both will suffer and eventually die. Small fish or creatures can become food for the axolotl but not before they have had a chance to pick at the axolotl's gills or fins. Axolotls are much happier all by themselves.

## 45. Can I keep a goldfish with an axolotl in the same tank?

It is a bad idea to keep goldfish and axolotl in the same tank. The goldfish may be gobbled up by the axolotl and before that happens, it may have nibbled at the axolotl's gills causing distress. Each requires different water temperatures. Lights cause stress in the axolotl while the goldfish welcomes it. Goldfish also produce more ammonia that can be absorbed by sponge filters which is not safe for the axolotl. Keeping them in the same tank is all-around stressful for all three: you, the goldfish, and the axolotl.

## 46. What fish should I keep with an axolotl?

Axolotls aren't a friendly lot at all. They may eat

limbs off other axolotls if hungry enough: they do grow back, after all. But if you wish to keep other fish in your axolotl tank, then choose one which is either too fast or too big to become a meal or does not find the axolotl's feathery gills a tasty snack. Also, if it reproduces fast enough, the population will be kept in balance. Some good options are listed below.

· Golden skiffia

· Orange-finned danio

· White cloud mountain minnow

· Zebra danio

## 47. What diseases afflict axolotls?

Most diseases that axolotls in captivity suffer from are bacterial in nature. They become prone to bacterial infections due to poor husbandry. Other stresses may also affect their resistance. Sometimes their gills start to weaken. If this is not treated in time, this stress may lead to disease. Other than infection, axolotls recover well from other injuries mainly due to their remarkable ability to regenerate and regrow damaged parts.

In conclusion, I must say that if you're a pet lover with exotic tastes, do go for the axolotl. but before you do that, make sure you're allowed to keep the axolotl as a pet in your area of domicile. Be prepared for hours of joyful entertainment, that also at a minimum cost.

# References

What is an Axolotl and Their Habitat? | Bluereef Portsmouth (bluereefaquarium.co.uk)

*What is an axolotl and their habitat?: Bluereef Portsmouth.* Bluereef Portsmouth | Blue Reef Aquarium Portsmouth. (2020, October 30). Retrieved December 23, 2021, from https://www.bluereefaquarium.co.uk/portsmouth/blog/education/what-is-an-axolotl-and-why-are-they-endangered/

Axolotl (nationalgeographic.com)

*Axolotl: National geographic.* Animals. (n.d.). Retrieved December 23, 2021, from https://www.nationalgeographic.com/animals/amphibians/facts/axolotl

How to Pronounce Axolotl? (CORRECTLY) Meaning & Pronunciation - YouTube

YouTube. (2011). *YouTube.* Retrieved December 25, 2021, from https://www.youtube.com/watch?app=desktop&v=xZS6FAscZoc&feature=youtu.be.

Axolotl - Definition, Classification, Characteristics and Reproduction (vedantu.com)

Vedantu. (2021, July 5). *Axolotl.* VEDANTU. Retrieved December 25, 2021, from https://www.vedantu.com/animal/axolotl

Axolotls: The Adorable, Giant Salamanders of Mexico | Live Science

Rehm, J. (2019, September 19). *Axolotls: The adorable, giant salamanders of mexico.* LiveScience. Retrieved December 25, 2021, from https://www.livescience.com/axolotl-facts.html

Axolotls — kidcyber

*Axolotls.* kidcyber. (n.d.). Retrieved December 25, 2021, from
https://www.kidcyber.com.au/axolotls

 Axolotl Colors: 15 Types of Axolotl Morphs & Pictures - Everything
Reptiles

David, J., & says:, T.-san. (2021, January 26). *Axolotl colors: 15 types of Axolotl
Morphs & Pictures.* Everything Reptiles. Retrieved December 25, 2021, from
https://www.everythingreptiles.com/types-of-axolotl-colors/


18 Types of Axolotl Colors You Can Own (Axolotl Color Guide) -
ExoPetGuides

-, S., By, -, & Sunny. (2020, January 10). *18 types of axolotl colors you can own
(axolotl color guide).* ExoPetGuides. Retrieved December 25, 2021, from
https://exopetguides.com/axolotl/axolotl-colors/

Axolotl | San Diego Zoo Animals & Plants

*Axolotl.* San Diego Zoo Wildlife Alliance Animals and Plants. (n.d.).
Retrieved December 25, 2021, from
https://animals.sandiegozoo.org/animals/axolotl

Axolotl Life Cycle - Axolotl (google.com)

*Axolotl life cycle - axolotl.* Google Sites. (n.d.). Retrieved December 26, 2021,
from https://sites.google.com/site/axolotljc2013/axolotl-life-cycle

Axolotl Breeding - Reptiles Magazine

Clare, J., & Clare, A. U. T. H. O. R. J. (2020, June 3). *Axolotl breeding.*
Reptiles Magazine. Retrieved December 26, 2021, from
https://reptilesmagazine.com/axolotl-
breeding/#:~:text=Remove%20the%20eggs%20or%20the,hatch%20in%2
0about%2015%20days.

68 Axolotl Facts: Ultimate Guide to the Adorable Mexican Walking Fish -
Everywhere Wild

Drew Haines (2021, May 3). *68 axolotl facts: Ultimate guide to the adorable Mexican walking fish*. Everywhere Wild. Retrieved December 26, 2021, from https://everywherewild.com/axolotl/#:~:text=To%20humans%2C%20ax olotls%20are%20a,axolotls%20can%20be%20quite%20dangerous.

Axolotl Life Cycle - Axolotl (google.com)

*Axolotl life cycle - axolotl*. Google Sites. (n.d.). Retrieved December 26, 2021, from https://sites.google.com/site/axolotljc2013/axolotl-life-cycle

Axolotl Facts (Ambystoma mexicanum) (thoughtco.com)

Anne Marie Helmenstine, P. D. (2019, April 2). *Axolotl? we've got a lot of answers*. ThoughtCo. Retrieved December 26, 2021, from https://www.thoughtco.com/axolotl-ambystoma-mexicanum-4162033

5 Weird but Normal Axolotl Behaviors - PetHelpful

H, J. (2020, December 10). *5 weird but normal axolotl behaviors*. PetHelpful. Retrieved December 26, 2021, from https://pethelpful.com/exotic-pets/5-Weird-but-Normal-Axolotl-Behaviors

https://www.northwoodspets.com/all-about-axolotls/

*Google scholar*. (n.d.). Retrieved December 26, 2021, from http://scholar.google.ca/

All About Axolotls - (northwoodspets.com)

*All about Axolotls*. Northwoods Pets. (n.d.). Retrieved December 26, 2021, from https://www.northwoodspets.com/all-about-axolotls/

Keeping and Caring for Axolotls as Pets (thesprucepets.com)

Lianne McLeod, D. V. M. (2021, December 20). *Keeping and caring for axolotls as pets*. The Spruce Pets. Retrieved December 26, 2021, from https://www.thesprucepets.com/axolotls-as-pets-1236714

How Much Does an Axolotl Cost? (2021 Price Guide) | Pet Keen

outdoorsman, D. E. A. avid. (2021, September 17). *How much does an axolotl cost? (2021 Price Guide)*. Pet Keen. Retrieved December 26, 2021, from https://petkeen.com/axolotl-cost/

Why are Axolotls Illegal to Own in Some States and Provinces? (axolotlcentral.com)

Sordillo, S. (2021, October 5). *Why are axolotls illegal to own in some states and provinces?* Axolotl Central. Retrieved December 26, 2021, from https://www.axolotlcentral.com/post/why-are-axolotls-illegal-to-own-in-some-states-provinces

Axolotl - Earth Day

*Axolotl.* Earth Day. (2020, April 22). Retrieved December 26, 2021, from https://www.earthday.org/axolotl/

Hope for the Axolotl (mit.edu)

*Hope for the axolotl.* science cow. (n.d.). Retrieved December 26, 2021, from http://sciencecow.mit.edu/MITblogs/axolotl.html#:~:text=Today%20there%20are%20estimated%20to,of%20what%20little%20habitat%20remains.

Axolotl Facts (softschools.com)

*Axolotl facts.* Math. (n.d.). Retrieved December 26, 2021, from https://www.softschools.com/facts/animals/axolotl_facts/256/

68 Axolotl Facts: Ultimate Guide to the Adorable Mexican Walking Fish - Everywhere Wild

Drew Haines (2021, May 3). *68 axolotl facts: Ultimate guide to the adorable Mexican walking fish.* Everywhere Wild. Retrieved December 26, 2021, from https://everywherewild.com/axolotl/

Axolotl - Description, Habitat, Image, Diet, and Interesting Facts (animals.net)

Team, A. N., & Oldham, C. (2018, May 27). *Axolotl - description, habitat, image, diet, and interesting facts.* Animals Network. Retrieved December 26, 2021, from https://animals.net/axolotl/#:~:text=The%20axolotl%20is%20a%20carnivore,and%20commercially-purchased%20salmon%20pellets.

Axolotl - Description, Habitat, Image, Diet, and Interesting Facts (animals.net)

Team, A. N., & Oldham, C. (2018, May 27). *Axolotl - description, habitat, image, diet, and interesting facts.* Animals Network. Retrieved December 26, 2021, from https://animals.net/axolotl/

How Often To Feed Axolotl [Owners Complete Feeding Guide] (peteducate.com)

Jeremy, & JeremyI am a practiced pet owner with decades of experience owning a number of different pets. I am also the main writer and chief editor here at Pet Educate; a site I created to share everything I've learned about pet ownership over the years and my exte. (2021, February 15). *How often to feed axolotl [owners complete feeding guide].* Pet Educate. Retrieved December 26, 2021, from https://peteducate.com/how-often-to-feed-axolotl/#:~:text=So%2C%20how%20often%20do%20you,it%20in%20the%20water%20nearby.

Axolotls - Frequently Asked Questions

*Frequently asked questions.* Axolotls - Frequently Asked Questions. (n.d.). Retrieved December 26, 2021, from https://www.axolotl.org/faq.htm

Axolotl | San Diego Zoo Animals & Plants

*Axolotl.* San Diego Zoo Wildlife Alliance Animals and Plants. (n.d.). Retrieved December 26, 2021, from https://animals.sandiegozoo.org/animals/axolotl#:~:text=The%20axolotl%20has%20few%20predators,lakes%20and%20ponds%20they%20inhabit.

How to look after an Axolotl | Kellyville Pets

*How to look after an axolotl.* Kellyville Pets. (n.d.). Retrieved December 26, 2021, from https://www.kellyvillepets.com.au/pages/how-to-look-after-an-axolotl-kellyville-pets

Axolotl Tank Decor, Hides and Plants | Exotic PetQuarters

Admroot. (2020, December 11). *Axolotl tank decor, hides and plants: Exotic petquarters.* Exotic PetQuarters |. Retrieved December 26, 2021, from https://exoticpetquarters.com/axolotl-care-sheet/axolotl-tank-decor-hides-plants/

Can You Hold An Axolotl? How to Safely Handle Your Axolotl | It's A Fish Thing (itsafishthing.com)

*Can you hold an axolotl? how to safely handle your axolotl.* It's A Fish Thing. (2021, March 26). Retrieved December 26, 2021, from https://www.itsafishthing.com/can-you-hold-an-axolotl/

Can Axolotls Breathe Out Of Water? [How Long Can They Be Out?] (peteducate.com)

Jeremy, & JeremyI am a practiced pet owner with decades of experience owning a number of different pets. I am also the main writer and chief editor here at Pet Educate; a site I created to share everything I've learned about pet ownership over the years and my exte. (2021, March 1). *Can Axolotls breathe out of water? [how long can they be out?].* Pet Educate. Retrieved December 26, 2021, from https://peteducate.com/can-axolotls-breathe-out-of-water/

The effect of cold on Axolotls. - Carolina Axolotls | Facebook

*Log into Facebook.* Facebook. (n.d.). Retrieved December 26, 2021, from https://m.facebook.com/Carolinaaxolotls/posts/the-effect-of-cold-on-axolotls/787983091709186/?_rdr

Do Axolotls Sleep? [It's Not As Clear-Cut As You Might Think] (peteducate.com)

Jeremy, & JeremyI am a practiced pet owner with decades of experience owning a number of different pets. I am also the main writer and chief editor here at Pet Educate; a site I created to share everything I've learned about pet ownership over the years and my exte. (2021, March 5). *Do axolotls sleep? [it's not as clear-cut as you might think].* Pet Educate. Retrieved December 26, 2021, from https://peteducate.com/do-axolotls-sleep/

\Why did My Axolotl Die? 8 Most Common Reasons 8 Common Reasons of Dead Axolotl - Axolotl Nerd

29, A. M. S., 10, A. N. N., & 25, F. T. A. M. A. (2020, November 4). *Why did my axolotl die? 8 most common reasons 8 common reasons of Dead Axolotl.* Axolotl Nerd. Retrieved December 26, 2021, from https://axolotlnerd.com/axolotl-died/

Can axolotls live with fish? [Axolotls tank mates guide] | Exopetguides

-, S. (2019, December 2). *Can Axolotls live with fish? [Axolotls Tank Mates Guide].* ExoPetGuides. Retrieved December 26, 2021, from https://exopetguides.com/axolotl/axolotls-tank-mates-guide/#:~:text=Axolotls%20certainly%20can%20live%20with,will%20suffer%20or%20die%20eventually.&text=Firstly%2C%20smaller%20sea%20creatures%20or,away%20your%20axolotls%27%20gills%20too.

Can goldfish live with axolotl? - Quora

*Can goldfish live with axolotl?* Quora. (n.d.). Retrieved December 26, 2021, from https://www.quora.com/Can-goldfish-live-with-axolotl

Axolotl tankmates: fish edition – Water Critters

Gen. (2019, March 27). *Axolotl tankmates: Fish edition.* Water Critters. Retrieved December 26, 2021, from https://www.watercritters.ca/2019/03/22/axolotl-tankmates/

Ask the Vet: Are you curious about the Axolotl? | Wollondilly Advertiser | Picton, NSW

*Ask the vet: Are you curious about the axolotl?* Wollondilly Advertiser. (2015, February 19). Retrieved December 26, 2021, from https://www.wollondillyadvertiser.com.au/story/2894003/ask-the-vet-are-you-curious-about-the-axolotl/

https://tardigrade.in/question/which-of-the-following-are-correct-for-axolotl-larva-i-it-shows-2ypomdl0

*Which of the following are correct for axolotl larva? (I) it.* Tardigrade. (n.d.). Retrieved December 27, 2021, from https://tardigrade.in/question/which-of-the-following-are-correct-for-axolotl-larva-i-it-shows-2ypomdl0

Made in the USA
Monee, IL
02 March 2024

54371600R00020